am•phib•ian

am•phib•ian

by

Jessica Lanay

BROADSIDE LOTUS PRESS
Detroit

Broadside Lotus Press

Publishers since 1965

First Edition

Printed in the United States of America

Cover Art, *Charybdis,* by Jessica Lanay

Concrete Poem Designs by Jessica Lanay

Cover and Book Layout by Leisia Duskin

NLM Award Series Editor: Gloria A. House

ISBN 978-0-940713-28-4

Broadside Lotus Press

Post Office 02011

Detroit, Michigan 48202

www.BroadsideLotusPress.org

ACKNOWLEDGMENTS

First, I want to thank my mother for always being the helium in my balloon, for growing with me in all directions.

I want to thank my great grandmother, Willie Lee Neal, the Key Lime Pie Lady of Key West. I want to thank my great grandfather Roosevelt Neal. They both remain my compass in this life. I want to thank my sister-cousin Erica, my auntie-mommy Theresa, my auntie-mommy Ida Mae (may she rest in peace and love), my grandma Peggy (for reminding me to scream and shout), and my great uncle Julius "Buddy" Adams, for his constant love.

And the land. I thank Key West, I thank 307 Cross Street, I thank 224 Truman, I thank the roses that were in my auntie-mommy Ida Mae's front yard on 11th Ave—for hiding me.

I want to thank my great grandmother Willie Lee's best friend, David Wolkowsky, for being family, for being there for her when she couldn't be there for herself.

And thank you to my extended family:

Thank you, Britain Gadsden, for the text every morning, for more than 15 years of friendship. When I was in the dark you lit a candle; when I was blind you made song and clapped. To Essence London—for everything, everything. To Yolanda "Get Your Gun" Franklin, for coaxing out my fearlessness. To Karen Brown, my lovely friend, my brilliant composer—thank you for expanding the universe where my words live. To Ariana Brown, for protecting me from my weaker self when I was done, and for loving her until I was ready to carry her. To Malcolm Friend, *hermanito mio*. To Josh, for bringing me clarity and joy. To Amy Feltman, for being there in the beginning. Thank you to Dianca London for reminding me that I am capable. Thank you to S. Erin for your vulnerability and love. To my witch, Blue June. Thank you to my sister, Oceana. I would pay my last to watch you dance. Thank you, Tío Rafa, for looking out for me since I was 18. You've stuck with me through my bad behavior. To Reginald Walker, for stepping up.

To my Hill District and Pittsburgh family:

Ms. Frankie, you show me every day how to love and accept myself more. Lakeisha Wolf, your work amazes me. Thank you to Ms. Sheila McDaniel, Geneva Jackson, Myra Hill, Cozetta Newring, Anna Pearl Spotwood, Jackie Halloway, Jo-Anne Bates, Bonita Lee Penn, and Sheila Carter-Jones. You all showed me just how to *be*.

To my manuscript family:

Thank you, Toi Derricotte. Your poetry gave me permission to not ask for permission. Thank you, Lynn Emanuel, for being such a great reader and poet. Thank you for returning, thank you for your faith in my work. Thank you to Dr. Jules Gill-Peterson, for empowering me, conspiring with me, supporting me, and introducing me to Dr. Ferenczi. Thank you, John Hennessy. Your generosity, your advice, your edits, your confidence, your friendship, make a difference in me as a writer and a person. Saint Paul Kameen, all of your compassion, knowledge, and truth kept me sane; thank you for warrioring at my side when I needed it. Thank you to Piotr Gwiazda. You went through every sentence, every comma, you found inspiration for me, you showed me what I could not see, you changed how I see myself as a writer. Thank you to Yona Harvey, for your honesty, vulnerability, kindness, and openness. Thank you to Peter Trachtenberg, for hacking my brain into this title (so sneaky!), for listening to me when things were tough. Thank you to Bhanu Kapil, for reminding me that I may dare to shapeshift. Thank you to Chris Abani, for carving out the time and space in your brain to help me break open the poems that led to the first section of this book.

And thank you to Dudley Randall and Naomi Long Madgett, for leaving behind your writing, legacies, and Broadside Lotus Press. Thank you, Dr. Gloria House, for your patience. Thank you, Wayne State University Press. Thank you, Cave Canem. Thank you, Millay Colony, where I built the bones of this manuscript. Calliope—you're a force. Thank you to Kimbilio.

Thank you all for coming into my life or helping me survive this manuscript or helping save the part of me that wrote it.

A gigantic thank you to the following journals for previous publication of the following poems:

The Common
"First Fall," "Mouthpiece," "A Brief History of Shrinking," "Dear Mountain," "Gills," and "Hex"

Poet Lore
"Junk Science"

Prairie Schooner
"A Tipsy Walk through the Night"

Fugue
"miracle : promise : cure : charm : votive : carry your altar.," and "Black Girl Notes on/to Sándor Ferenczi"

DEDICATION

For my mommy, Rose Renee Neal.
No one can tell us it did not happen anymore.
For my great grandmother, my small goddess, Willie Lee Neal,
and my great grandfather, the love of my life, Roosevelt Neal.
Without you, I would not have lived this long.

Contents

III

IV

V

I

Lilliput

When you died I wanted to know everything
about dandelions

the lilliputian flowers

silver
fiber
bursts

attached

to the same base

every umbrella seed

identical

mirror after mirror

we were like this once
weren't we like this?

before the wind

Please.

Tell me we were.

Topo

I.
The land's clock is the water   everything bright flame
     losing oxygen   losing   growing from face
high to the orange tongues of green beasts   to tall
enough to drive the trolleys   never having to learn the
names of your lanes   the sea ululating hunger a white noise

II.
When the roots cannot suck through the stone   they go
up   they speak double   up-up   high-high   wooden
tarantulas   they've known the island since the ocean
was teething   equivalency   which island disappeared   so
where I was born could be born   Hy'Brasil maybe

III.
There are more dead here than people   you learn to prefer it   so
     the Poinciana blushes to blood   giving red
shade   wind chimes of sun   this heat is unbearable
leaving sea water on our graves is unbearable   a man in white
     walks from between the stacked graves   no one else
sees him   no one else sees anything   we could not see
the eclipse from the island   in this way   we are outside-outside
     what rules does your death have?

IV.
Iguanas burst open   a run over orange   heart askew   limbs
     a new gesture   a stamp on the hot road they may
belong to Uncle Bucca   who raises them   sets them free
they aren't pets he insists   *pets you keep from dying*
a person can be an absent god   of just   about anything

V.
I was weighed here   so to speak   first broke my head
on the elephantine limb of this ceiba   weighed
a heart in the duat   you must pass through trials   only
to end up   looking at a feathered god   on an island in   eternity
if you are too heavy   you are cast into   oblivion
your soul gathers filth   clothes gather filth
     one can be washed   one can't   weighed   a fruit   a feather
did you come here looking for biography?   did you come
     looking for release?   I have none for you
I don't come from anyone that maps such things.

Black Box

The heat of his mouth softens the wax. Each wan wing is painstakingly layered to wick away the wind's tears. Expectation is a guard that may or may not be blind. My song calls the birds
moulting   freedoms   individua l   what does obsessive toil do to love   had he a
son   had he a daughter   in mythology   remembered   for much
too much
too long
when does it stop mattering   if Daedalus   had a daughter
or a son   whether he was   an engineer   or   a pilot   he named me
after   where I fell   an ocean   named me   nothing
Ikaros   *Icarus*   *Icaria*   an ocean
an ungendered thing   a pilot   an engineer
love gathering   conditions   like weather
not too low   salt eats   not to high   sun burns
forbid me   a daughter   that navigates   that is of both
to know better   his black box
in case his craft   falls to the ocean
made after him   in many ways
a fiction burst from the egg
of his mind   a fulfillment
umbilical cord   of intellect   of never enough
he never turned when the only one
who could affirm his horrors   I   tumbled   half melted
from the sky   his black box

e
j
e
c
t
i
n
g
t
o
s
e
a

my head recording   his voice   *mayday*   my chest   sunken hull holding
his flight path   I   she   falls   to my mother   the place   that
gave   my name   definition   I learn   how to swim
what   happened   my wings   gave way
to gills   became   a new   creature   his memory
lost   to salt   my body   translating   to nymphs
seafoam   spreading   like   a   burst whale   ocean
keeping my blood   ever living

Cloud Reader

No matter what you do   father   I answer   in a tone of unreasonable happiness
every attempt at talking   like stepping into a puddle   deeper than expected

Weather weather weather   this is how you respond to   *how are you*   or   *how do you feel*
You wanted to be a pilot but became a mechanic   you say because you broke your ankle

Of course you wanted the sky   the horizon is as good a destination as any
when you come from a brown beach town   where your mother lost her childhood

behind a Dairy Queen on Cleveland Avenue   when it was a dirt road   your father
a man who did not say he loved you   until you were fifty   of course   you wanted

the sky   I joke about my inheritances: your shitty ankles   your premature white hair
your white liver   you laugh through your nose   *attagirl*   everything I want to say

holds still and patiently waits   a stinging thing   in a desert   tail twitching
you quiz me   *what is cirrocumulus*   you are fluent in sky   over 6,000 miles a dead sea

I hear you are drunk   pink-faced and lanky   a flamingo   I play along
Clouds that fall apart and never reach the ground and rain in like, I don't know, eight hours?

that's my girl   I see my mother body splayed   falling from the sky
away from you   dissipating over me   how do you define remembering

a thing is pulverized if it falls far enough   you ask *tell me everything*
I do: *my lover cheated on me*   *grabbed my throat*   *wrung me*   *put a knife*

in my face and declared   *that his love is such*   *that he would kill me*   *first*
you did these things too   you must know how   they come to be you say

some stuff you can't forgive   *like getting on an elevatoror*   *a jet*   *the sky*
is made to let you fall   *that's all I know*   *that's all I know about love*

briefly   I am falling   levitating out of my seat   weightless
a drop   splitting the blue   a wayward body   the rest of me

to the sea

Bouquets

For a while   mother   I was the fish inside you   tumbling over myself
centrifugal
You often say   *you saved me*   this allegiance
whenever your father touched my stomach you moved away from his hand
imagine
me darting towards a corner in your blood reef
I make sure your house   is an altar choked with roses   orchids
flores de paraiso
offerings   a devout   woman tosses   to a sea goddess
you look
you have a mirror   on   every   wall   your bed   surrounded
by every valuable thing   you own   each mirror a well   reflections crossing
you look
we stand naked   before the glass   our bodies
share slopes curvatures dimples paunches
you look
all the black spots   on you   that will never turn   brown again
although you left   my father   fifteen years ago
we get dressed   you pull my collar   find that I am two roses short
my own bouquet   of never fading flowers   in some ways
we are not alike   there is only one mirror   in my home

and I cannot stand it

I cannot look

I   know   what   I   look   like

First Fall

Lover, we dampened the cool white sheets,
throwing each other, knowing
we are both liars; we didn't get
what we wanted: me—a chest
to shelter me for the night; you—
some reassurance that you had any
power at all in the world.
We awoke and love abandoned
us on an island together.
We did not know what to do
with each other, we barely
knew each other's names;
smelling storm, we huddled like swallows,
making nests of each other's ribs.

Second Fall

When we fight, lover, we speak to people
who aren't there, to people we are not:
your mother who forgot you
like a pile of gray stones;
my father leaving me to crash
a black box of memory   into the sea
you raise your fist   gesture   the thinnest skin
is over the eyes   like my mother   I am a spear
I throw my body at you to remind myself
who I do not want to be; to remind you
to want me; to remind you that like
snapdragons, the seed from which my
blood grows is skull-shaped; to remind
you that I, too, possess a violence.

Mouthpiece

I hear   the difference   your tongue   muting some words
    a bird with a chipped beak   the song lacking a note   an absence   I say   *I know*
it hurts I am sorry I am sorry   these are the physics   of cruelty
    expecting brutality   for small   or no   mistakes
the physics   of being   the lake that catches   the rain   the dashed
    I make room for you   to collapse into me
    sink   your mouth   broken canoe   our hair
    coarse seaweed   remaining teeth to points
    false wings to gills
    a lamentation   a pile of dry palmettos   burning crackling
for all the things   I can't correct   your body is an altar   crumbling
    no matter   how much   I speak of love   we are each the future
of women suspected   of killing their men   women who marched out of swamps
    with children who   only bore traces of their mothers   you remind me
of this lineage   when I confess   that my own lover   waits
until   I   am   not   looking

Dream

Tight-lipped, nothing to waste
not even a word
Secret swallower—cool as a yellowgray
snake shuddering tall grass
Where is that baby? Calling me
across the yard to show me something:
feed the hens this way, cut greens slant;
butterfly thumping
against the glass: my breath
one of the last things you remembered
was my name   the grief   of you
dying   roots upturned   sucking sky
transforming your children to gulls
a woman broken down enough turns to poison
your daughter died   before you
your granddaughter   died   at an age
younger than yours   at death
          turn   to   poison
anything done well is medicine
anything over done is poison

what   of   love   in   this   case

you too   are gone   but you leave me
with hexes on my breath
kai   kai   kai kai mi   me caí   me caí   kai mi
                                        split open my gills

Third Fall

Lover, we folded the clothes, and who knows
what I said or meant to say. You waited,
my back turned, you balled your fingers—
I fall so often, I fall so far. I beg you
for this when you are on top of me
but you refuse to do it then, maybe
this arena is different. You have found
me to be the animal that never abides.
I am still learning myself, that I take
no commands. You wait until
I lower my mouth to the water, until
I close my eyes in relief and sigh:
there is often a mountain between
what is said and what is received.

Fourth Fall

Tonight, lover, we are bright like silver
striking silver, I tasted her—
pulled her name off of your sex—saved
the photos before I woke you with blows.
I fall so heavy and so often and so far;
bruxing in my dreams; waking
with hematite in my mouth, I did
not flee our home in the black morning
because you fucked her—I scattered
like tortured doves—because you put the knife
to my mouth, as if it were a peach,
promised that you loved me enough
to make an open fruit of me, said,
you first and then myself.

Dream
(continued)

I knew no names to call
owned no bones to burn
how to conjure
broke against myself
surging pink salts
I was alone
walking across ice

the ice   my skin
broke   gave way
beneath I find your body
eel black   fishy eyes   turning
                flicking your tail
I awoke with a chest full
of names   purple stones
raven's lost beak
ask around our island
about you   they say   you just up
out of nowhere   say you killed
that white man   then ran
watching me kneel
under the hulk of this life

command me   *get up*
        get up
        heavy headed flower
loll   *in the wind*   *bite*
your photograph   your round face
your black hand holding river quartz
you say *spit and make rivers*
you say *scream up a mountain*
    dip your fingers in yourself
say you are that woman
talk backwards
she-wolf

        howl   *goddamnit*

Fifth Fall

We have licked each other to wound, lover,
worried ourselves like water
worries a stone   I hold up my hands
I hold up my hands   admit first   I have fallen
so far so heavy   I beg with palms flat
say   *this can kill me*   *this can kill me*
you left your seed in me without asking
I plead with chaos   make myself prone   beg
stop   your laughter   I fall   I fall
to the sea   to the sea   *kai*   *kai*
me caí   *kai*   *caí*   you burst
over me like hail *this can kill me*
you burst   over me a rogue thing
I beg   with palms flat   stop.

Final Fall

We both know this is done
mouth full of dandelion
of failed desire
whose throats must be stretched
down the wrong pipe
you beg me *say anything*
another name pinned
that name will salt
all names will salt
you will be betrayed
genuflecting lungs
you beg me *say anything*
my name piling
take to the water
my throat locked
to mask the scent of shame
I come from women
they swallow water
they have gills
I vomit stones of quiet
between your cheek and jaw
away to my name
away to my name
you will drown here
bricks of burning salt
I vomit stones of quiet
a rogue thing over your head
it is done

Hanged

torn a floral print dress flailing in a tree during a storm
a house on its side contents floating free
my body must come down watch the hawks sniffing blood
they say the worst is done the dying
my mother saves the nails the feathers
puts the gum of the wax in her mouth to chew
Daedalus you flew so far ahead
you could not tell the difference between my body
and sea foam broke rummaged by the sea
my inheritance is not sky I I I
dissolved in the quick
let me rest
without praying every little thing
will be known when my heart is weighed
against a feather my tongue a feather
glimmers but *please*
bring me down

Howl

It could not have added up to anything but this
I count what I know from a pocket with a hole

marching through the world flail chested fighting
a blade on each breeze   back to the bright

rough howling   horns thrashing   every seed
carries the permutations of blooms that preceded it

what to do when you awake to life and find
yourself a composite of strange beasts

find you are not only the battlefield but the soldier
not only the soldier but the weapon

not only the weapon but the armor
all those things   and   the enemy

what a dream   what a conjuring   the mauled
and meager that make you up throwing

in what is left of their flesh   a meal for the starving
I want to rain into the sea   be the cycle dissipating

I spit and make a river
I scream up a mountain

I place my fingers in myself and say I am this woman
I talk backwards and scatter the men

I rain   dissipate   fall
poison   then   medicine

I got up and howled

Goddamnit

Shudder, Clink I

I shudder I clink I shrink to think that this is grief one long wire between all the rooms heating all spaces where other things may live warming my creatures of joy or even my creatures of sadness a spore in the skiff of a red blood cell surfing fast through the thin skin of my life I shudder I clink I shrink to think that this is grief the white paint on all the walls in all the rooms that face the common hall with their locked doors the body like a house each room each organ discrete but if one deteriorates then all ashens to the bone I shudder I clink I shrink to think that this is grief a sudden artificial light

II

Lilliput

everything

silver

we were like this

when you died I wanted to know

about dandelions

lilliputian
flowers fibers

attached

bursts

each umbrella
seed identical

to one another
mirror
after
mirror
Weren't we like this?

before the wind
Please
tell me we were.

Scylla

There is a day drawing near   when I will be the only one left
of my kind   the already dead   come to me

o my heart which I have from my mother

            o my eyes which I have from her sister

I crawl onto land   wheezing on my belly   survived

            I number my dead   like new or rare plants

and know love

Abreaction I

My anger—springs from its haunches from two directly to seven.

At what level is excommunication? At what level is pride? At what level is excessive love, lust? I envision a mountain goat cleaving hooves to a cliff, scared of being let go.

In every room of me there is a reminder of the beauty in being proficient at attacking.

I map the in-between in white chalk marks in the shape of my body. Be quiet, listen to myself. I hear the rain rattle in the sky before it plummets to the ground. I hear water ping the void in me where all the dead women I am afraid to become are resting.

I cannot speak of myself without speaking of sea beasts.

A Brief History of Shrinking

In the history of Dido, she killed herself to avoid getting married—not because Aeneas left her. He is not even real. She might have lived one hundred years before Virgil invented him. But a conquest is not complete without a woman who kills herself for a love that is only an illusion.

You will never be married or God bless the man who chooses you. Those words, peppered over my head by my aunts and mother, when as a child in a red jumper and canvas shoes I cursed my father. I have the right to curse him, he is a cursable man.

That is the extravagance of blood: the hardness of his grandfather, and blank unkindness of his father passing through him into his small daughter. The truest inheritances are these mythologies.

Virgil made Dido a composite of what he considered empire-wrecking women. In order to write a history of valiant men, he drew Dido as Cleopatra, as Calypso: abandoned, forgotten, and/or dead—erased from any stele.

My mother is the only woman in my family that left her husband and stayed gone. But not before I learned the violence of watching her be unloved for no reason at all.

The other women in my family died in their late sixties. Their men, who they locked their jaws around, continued their unconditional devotion to doing whatever they pleased into their nineties, despite the fact that their carelessness killed their women.

When the men are buried, they are piled into the columbarium with the women's bodies that—even in decomposition—shrink to leave just enough room to be climbed on top of.

Seven Facts About Octopuses

1. Should I ask my mother if she is lonely?

Female octopuses, when they are protecting their deep sea nurseries, turn themselves inside out.

2. Once she began telling me a story about Rick James, and it sounded like she knew him. I was really quiet, still, like I would scare her away. I wanted to ask her what Rick James was like in person. Should I have asked her?

Octopuses have three hearts. One stops beating when they swim.

3. In a rush to leave the house, she kneels on all fours, tossing shoes over her shoulder. Designer leather straps and hand-formed heels pile up. Our features are identical, but I am the color of wet sand, like my father. I want to ask her why she chose that white man.

Octopuses are able to change the color of their entire body in three-tenths of a second. By controlling the density of their melanin, they can change their colors to orange, yellow, purple, blue....

4. She tries to make me wear pink. She tries to make me comb my hair. I am as fraudulent as ever, but it makes her happy. What am I supposed to get out of this? What did she get out of it?

Even when severed, octopuses' arms react, pulling away when pinched. Two-thirds of their brain's neurons reside in their tentacles.

5. I want to ask my mother how to be alone, how to lessen my body's tendency to be lonely.

Female octopuses die after mating. They retreat to lairs where they lay their eggs and guard them until they hatch. They lose strength as they fend off predators, stop eating, and then slowly go through cellular suicide.

6. I show my mother how to accentuate her peak with liquid lipstick. I make two mountains and then fill in a tight bow. She knows how to do this but still demands I show her. Why?

Octopuses use their ink to disable their prey. However, the ink also contains an enzyme called tyrosinase, which causes blinding irritation when it gets into another animal's eyes.

7. Her "boyfriend" comes over by mistake. She says he is spying. I peek through the window and I hear him say, "I just want to know more about you." She sighs in the driveway, tells him to leave. I want to ask if she's ever confused peace for loneliness or loneliness for peace.

Octopuses love to be alone.

For the Birds

Enough. What is it with writers and birds. I try to reason out of my obsession. I suppose that birds should only be the hollow-boned shit machines that they are. How much more can you put on their fragile little backs before finding them crushed at the foot of some building's stoop? I come from a place and such a time that the land makes people free the exotic birds they trapped. The opaline white cockatoo, the primary colored macaw, on the clotheslines, shitting on your clean laundry, repeating the argument from last night. *Why didn't you put the fucking meat in the icebox, nah?* I come from a place and such a time that when I am forty, all of my elders will be dead: how many things to do on an island? How many birds? How many ways to die? The futility of the pastime of wishing one was a bird—they are so much older than us, by millions of years.

In cages spray-painted turquoise and gold, we kept parakeets. It was my job to sweep and scrub their shit from the floor. My mother brought home ginger jars decorated with birds outlined in silver. I hid things in them—secrets or poems, I can't remember—on slips of paper. I tried to draw the birds, cement them down in rendering, then put those bodies, those secrets, in the jars. Most birds swallow their prey whole—like snakes. A snake is mostly muscle. A bird is mostly air. I am mostly water, but cannot live in my complementary environment.

The birds never lasted long in my home. Not with older brothers silvering the live ones with spray paint. Not with the jars on which the others lived giving into the thoughtless movement of bodies—struggling. I found them dead at the bottom of their cages; dead on the floor. The last bird, Papi, tore his blue feathers and pink skin on his neck. I put on a garden glove, took him from his cage, went out onto the back porch, and squeezed him until he popped. *Why don't you throw that thing away*, asks my mother. I planned to bury him, but I threw him away.

Junk Science

Dedicated to my Uncle Junior. May he rest in peace.

The ocean cycles   you will be a starfish   someday
I am concerned with what the body does in life   how it decides
Indeed   it decides without consulting
        maybe it does   and a person doesn't listen
A man enters the E.R. with a lawnmower blade stuck in his head
They don't remove it   the gray matter is already operating under its new condition
Some injuries hold shit together
My great uncle presses my fingers into the side of his thigh
I feel the edges of a war artifact inside of him
He touches the shrapnel as his memory quietly packs itself away
There are several people around me losing their memory
        how merciful   enough already

I know what is slipping from their minds   better they forget
My great grandmother spent her life surviving on the dirt's possibilities
Garden of greens   chamomile   honey   garlic   for pink eye
Call me *bruja*
In a dream   I walk into the yellow house I grew up in   see my great grandmother
knees together   heels apart   her body a curl of ink in yellow chico slacks
La Lupe is on the television   slapping her own face   *mandingo coño*
My great grandmother   copies her movements
I realize   I am watching   an 80 year old woman   not a 15 year old girl
Watching her I know that some joy is small

        strange

            erotic

                mostly private

Abreaction II

Within moments I feel the tug, a pulley from the base of my head, to my tail-bone. Turning my chin to the right hurts. Hand heels pushing over the brows. Shake the inkling that if I could name these muscles they would heed. I need names to create maps, and what is that but a different bill of ownership. I want a tide map with a word for every ripple of this feeling so I can tell where it stops. But the ennui comes from behind my ears to the tips of my fingers. If you don't let it out—the pus will make its own way.

Loss takes efficient tolls, an actuary of the body. These losses: a fog stretching to the edges of my life. Giving me fins, contorting me to myth. My body starts grieving before my mind can count the absences around me. I take an accounting of all the holes.

Ida Mae I: Your Remains

Thin, gold,
silk headscarf.

Retired wedding ring
in a fake velvet bag.

Cackling seed pod
from the Poinciana.

Yellow, black, and red
boxes of Argo Starch.

Sparkly beauty supply
store slippers.

Black and white school photo,
circa 1963.

Swatch of honey
colored gingham.

Broken mirror in a ceramic
birth control cartridge.

Marbles that look
like your eyes, my eyes.

Watchtower magazines—
are you ready for the great beyond?

Cashmere cardigan with plastic
diamonds for buttons.

Jewel turquoise espresso cup
chipped down to white.

More boxes—yellow, red, black—
of Argo Starch.

When they call to say you are dead,
I lay against the ground.

They turn you to ash. Give you to the sea.

Ida Mae II

This is the church where you were married: the walls tall and white-washed, everything with prim blue trim, palm trees outside applauding. I never saw your wedding photos. Fifteen years ago, my mother ran from this island with me in tow. I return for the occasion of your death. At the front of the church, your photo in a plastic frame leans against your ashes in a plastic bag.

Girded by my uncles, I break like a jar of palm oil. Uncle Bucca, almost 100, twists his hands around my hand. My Uncle Lopez, his arm around me, pats my shoulder as rage rocks his body. Uncle Lopez is the man who loved you so poorly you did not know that the next man would kill you. Anything was better than Uncle Lopez. Still, the man you died under spent enough of your money—that you were burned—not buried.

People testify to your generosity, which they never returned. Your sister Ann, while still in the sanctuary, asks for the money she is owed for burning you. She shames my mother for not attending. White tourists poke their heads into the repast to ask what we are celebrating—although we are all dressed in black.

I am a shard of lifeboat, splintering from the ship of family. Once I light my lantern, after they throw you into the ocean, I will never speak to any of them again. My first memory always of playing in the pink and red roses you coaxed from the dirt in tropical heat on 11th Avenue—you keeping me like a mother, brushing my hair, us looking each other in the green eyes we share.

I learned memory is cruel and mostly changes events so someone can remember themselves a certain way, in a way that helps them survive themselves.

Ida Mae III: The Girl

you the girl you took the rose blistering with blushing yellow and pink with the cold i wonder if you ever thought of the bitter medicine of the stem in your tight eager palm the stigmata of almost every other girl and the things she must and the things she will never the tart cut of striped watermelon candy in the cheek the body ungrateful for what the damn rose must have meant coy nature coaxed from uncolorful conditions begging always for a hand did you know that like it you would be a pretty whorl rent from the dirt for a shirt lapel for coiffure to make something else beautiful with your beauty i know enough to know you said yes to ease yes to waste not yes to please expectations polished to look like good the uncanniness of the thing you became grabbed and also became overgrown against the aluminum fence the uncanniness of knowing that being an adornment is also a way of being adorned that there is no real shame in wanting to be in someone's hands i am trying to explain how it happens that the very essence of a she is an intentional kind of going missing

A Tipsy Walk through the Night

When auntie-mommy Ann walks out of the bathroom, she holds her breasts with one hand and uses her free hand to cover her punani. She runs across the room snickering and giggling at herself, her hips shuffling from side to side.

When you come out naked, you stand with your hands on your hips. You tilt your head to the side and make eye contact with whoever is there. And if no one is there, then you look at yourself in the mirror. Your whole body forming the word "there."

All of our stomachs protrude into fatty paunches before forming the pillow of our punani crowded between our thighs.

I've inherited both you and auntie's relative hairlessness. Auntie-mommy once joked in front of her third husband that it was our "French" blood; he's dead now.

When I walk out naked, I swing my arms at my side, and look into any vanishing point. Mother, you and I had different youths. Mine is much more cautious; I am a trapeze artist with a taut net. I've never met the men you've known, or had the kind of sex you've had, although we may have done the same drugs.

Both you and auntie's eyes scour my body when I leave the shower. You both say it is to *make sure* but neither of you tell me of what.

We take a tipsy walk towards Higgs Beach, so we can return to what we came from. The only lights on the island are the lights of passing cars, the drivers of which are surprised to see three naked Black women, scuttling like crabs out towards the sea.

Shudder, Clink II

on a spider's comfort reminding a list of all the things that can undo a web: wind a finger a winged bug decay the birth of my own ilk never knowing myself without the old limed taint of loss this horrific scale: when one hand is filled the other is emptied this conjure potion of rotten betraying insufficient text It enters it leaves it atrophies in a book's closed sternum I shudder I clink I shrink to think that this is grief hopping from one tale to the next but all the symbols are the same every fucking sky or cliche bird still whipping above my head I may contort I may implode around that self

III

Lilliput

when you died
I wanted to know
everything
liliputian flowers
about dandelions

silver
bursts
fiber

attached at the base
identical
mirror after mirror

every
umbrella
seed

tell me we were like this
before the wind
please
we were like this once

Split

I am Alice, or rather, an Alice. I am split, myself and Alice to keep me company through grief. I am Alice in the way that all lost girls are Alice. I hold out my finger, touch the silver skim of my imagination, polished until I see the whites of my eyes. No rabbit screaming I'm late, I'm late, I'm late. My memory a river walking backwards. I am on the wrong side of the world. Here, I think in cuneiform. Here, where do you come from is a rhetorical question. The answer is nothing : nowhere, like a sound seems to come from nothing : nowhere, then falls apart. Are you where you come from? Will I awake from this dream when the post-nasal drip tickles the back of my throat, cuts down my windpipe. The breath becoming a caesura surrounded by sounds of thirst then coughing. Too much river here. Say—I am from Laputa, strung up by magnetic fields. Say—I am from Houyhnhnms, where horses rule and train humans to take to all fours. Say—I am from a place that only communicates in images of ram-headed, dead, prayerbeat gods. Say—I jumped from your imagination or I fell into my imagination. Say—I am from Wonderland. How could you leave me here like this? Say—there is silence—if such a thing could be. I am from a place where I am too big and too small. I push my hand through the quicksand in my brain; am I safer here? How could you leave me nowhere? Now, I am forced to be both myself and Alice because I cannot do this alone. Will you come with me? Can you bear with me? Do you trust me enough to stop swimming with me? Alice, Alice, are you there? I am talking to you, we are almost there, we are falling. Maybe we can die here, and if we die here, will we wake? Am I approaching you or waving goodbye? Coming apart at the skin. The edge of the sky eating itself from starvation. Alice, drown with me. There is no other way. Our sound is becoming a stamp, a hieroglyph that keeps us from dissolving into water. The post nasal drip in my body is the last thing I felt. Alice, we are going to die in this dream, our last breath just about to say

Lost

Are you in the same world in which you have always been?

Sidewalk that seems to
s
  l
    o
  p
e   m
under your feet.   u
                                                i
                                                l
Every organ inside of you   e
a latex glove inflated with h

the church's spire
at eye level

Abandonment is the absence
                                                     u o
      r v t   r   n
of g   a   i   y—everything   a   d
                                                     you   b   o   b   b   i   n   g

                                                                                                                        a   w   a   y
You break like flint   o v e r   y e a r s
you've s c a t t e r e d
many wholes
to the w   n   d
                            i

through the glass
of your mind
a muffled cry
may sound like desire;
might be desire;
something that forms

a bestiary of tiny gods.

A note: to be the subject
          of a promise
          is to be the subject
          of nothing   at   all.

Hurricane

You always wondered if it is okay to be alone
too often. Now, you have no choice, Alice.
Best laid plans wear away at the edge.
You're toppling through your mind,
a darkness filled with light you cannot see.
I understand your desire to turn around,
but you cannot, nothing is changing,
but everything is changing. You have
the feeling of being neutrino phase,
just a particle, you shall fall right
through the earth. They would have
you call this melancholia, but
we know better. Alice, we have been
here before; The only
escape is falling to pieces.
Your body is a condemned
structure, a sinkhole. And
what creaturely gods will
your sadness take the
shape of? And what
beasts will crawl out of
your wound in the
early morning
to accompany
you in the
world that
now rests
o n
y o u r
t o n g
u e
l i k e
c h a
l k
?

Wandering

T h i n k
of the body as an anchor, Alice. To lose
is to be loosed. A new absence :
a wild wandering, in this way t h i n g s
and feelings go on forever. Almost like
stealing from yourself sometimes you never know
your intention until the thing is actually l o s t .
However you slice it, the lost object is an unwanted
character. It isn't your fault, you can't help it: your state of
mind. Think of children in grocery stores—how they lose
themselves and end up sitting in front with a red balloon on
their wrist. Sleep walking from your bed to your s e c o n d
story porch after you attack the clothes on the h a n g e r .
Who are you running from? Who hurt you through forgetting
you were there? You peer into the seam of yourself,
pulling apart the sides to see the light moving, viscous. In
a dream you are pregnant, and although they say this means
happiness, you beat on the bulge until you are sunflower
oil on the floor. Then you slip and fall in your own
mess. You misplaced your yellow raincoat, you
didn't even realize it. *The unconscious makes*
use of favorable moments: you walked to
the edge without feeling the height
or awaking. Although
you promised,
you
never
called
to make amends. Tie a red balloon on your arm and pray someone finds you.

Nells Ghost

But this glimmer, this condensation follows you until one day on the toilet you say in its direction, "You can't be all the way in the world with your nose turned up like that."

At first, you think there is a floater in your eye: thin inclusion passing over your iris. A doctor in a lab coat tells you about an Iranian astronomer named Hasan Ibn al-Haytham. She peers into you with high powered glass, says *Light does not come from within us, you know.* You find you can still see the silvery flash, like a horse, galloping out of the corner of your eye.

You move out of the way of nothing on empty streets.

You cannot distinguish the movement from a sound come to run you down. Maybepsychosomatic—a poltergeist of your suspicion or your loneliness; it never arrives. The flare hangs out near the ceiling—a silver blimp caught in the duststatic in the corner. Your imagination is quite unruly. It rules everything in your body: the most desperate, pathetic monster.

Pool of Tears/ Evaporation

T
h e
s h o r e
behind is not
so useful the
lights only mean
something if we
give them
names

D
e a r
A l i c e ,
what will you
do when your
m i d - s e a s k i f f
slips out from
u n d e r
you?

res
c u e
does not
mean that
you will not
drown but how
else will you
get your new
gills?

h
o w
else will
you cross all
of this sea and
storm break the
waves and survive
on bitter sea
foam?

Tea Time

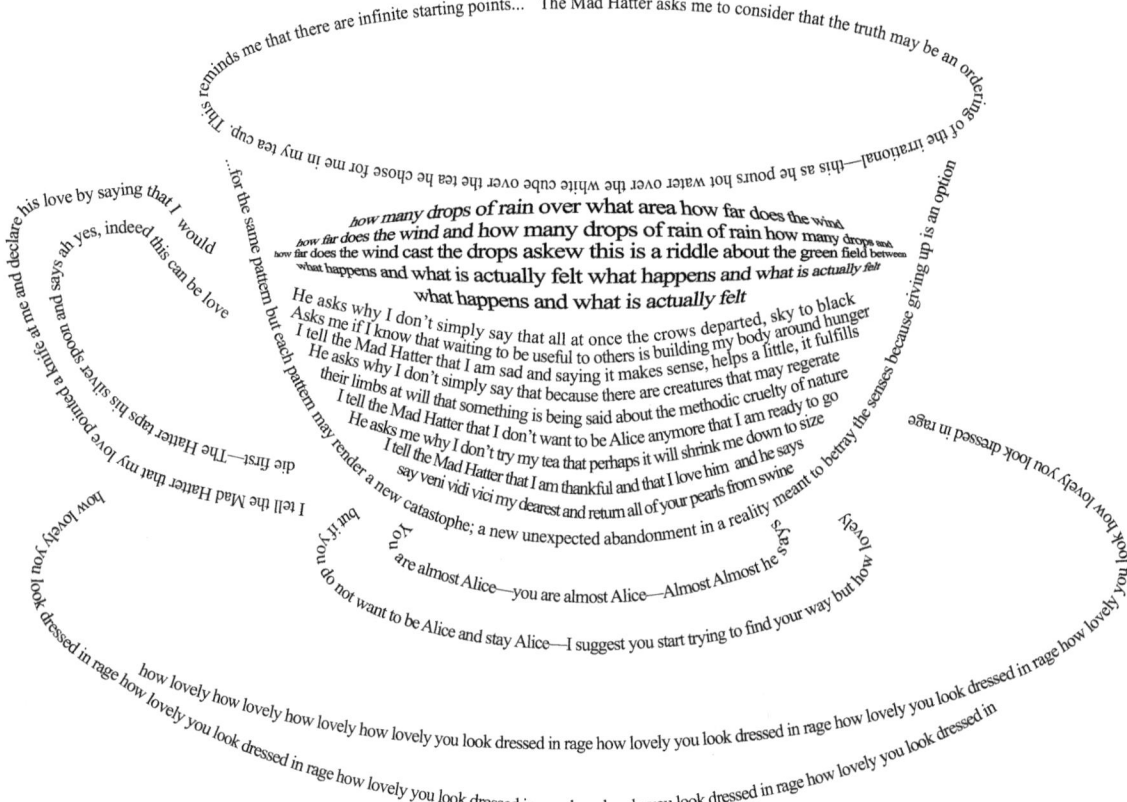

The Mad Hatter asks me to consider that the truth may be an ordering of the irrational—this as he pours hot water over the white cube over the tea he chose for me in my tea cup. This reminds me that there are infinite starting points...

...for the same pattern but each pattern may render a new catastophe; a new unexpected abandonment in a reality meant to betray the senses because giving up is an option

how many drops of rain over what area how far does the wind
how far does the wind and how many drops of rain of rain how many drops and
how far does the wind cast the drops askew this is a riddle about the green field between
what happens and what is actually felt what happens and *what is actually felt*
what happens and what is actually *felt*

He asks why I don't simply say that all at once the crows departed, sky to black
Asks me if I know that waiting to be useful to others is building my body around hunger
I tell the Mad Hatter that I am sad and saying it makes sense, helps a little, it fulfills
He asks why I don't simply say that because there are creatures that may regerate
their limbs at will that something is being said about the methodic cruelty of nature
I tell the Mad Hatter that I don't want to be Alice anymore that I am ready to go
He asks me why I don't try my tea that perhaps it will shrink me down to size
I tell the Mad Hatter that I am thankful and that I love him and he says
say veni vidi vici my dearest and return all of your pearls from swine

You are almost Alice—you are almost Alice—Almost Almost he says

but if you do not want to be Alice and stay Alice—I suggest you start trying to find your way but how lovely

I tell the Mad Hatter that my love pointed a knife at me and declare his love by saying that I would die first—The Hatter taps his silver spoon and says ah yes, indeed this can be love

how lovely you look dressed in rage how lovely you look dressed in rage how lovely you look dressed in rage how lovely you look dressed in rage how lovely you look dressed in rage how lovely you look dressed in

how lovely how lovely how lovely how lovely how lovely you look dressed in rage how lovely you look dressed in rage how lovely you look dressed in rage how lovely you look how lovely you look dressed in rage

Returned

m
a
e
r
You won't get it d your things
this is the price r e t u r n e d
it will always cost a little everytime
pack off your back you are finally leaving
through the ajar door you don't and won't go back
with a terrible headache wake up in bed
the frosted window and hunger through and through
a frightened flock you all apples on the ground
are so hungry so hungry pain is doppler echoing
so hungry after just a bite you are so humilitated
I have to say goodbye you can't take anymore
You are old skin our need is not mutual
apples on your tongue awake with the taste of milk
all the uneaten apples forgive yourself please
to take care sometimes you had to be away
a cloud nor a period this means to split neither
you made it nor a landscape nor
to the next step d r o w n i n g
s w i m m i n g w i t h o u t
ever dying

Riddle/Conundrum

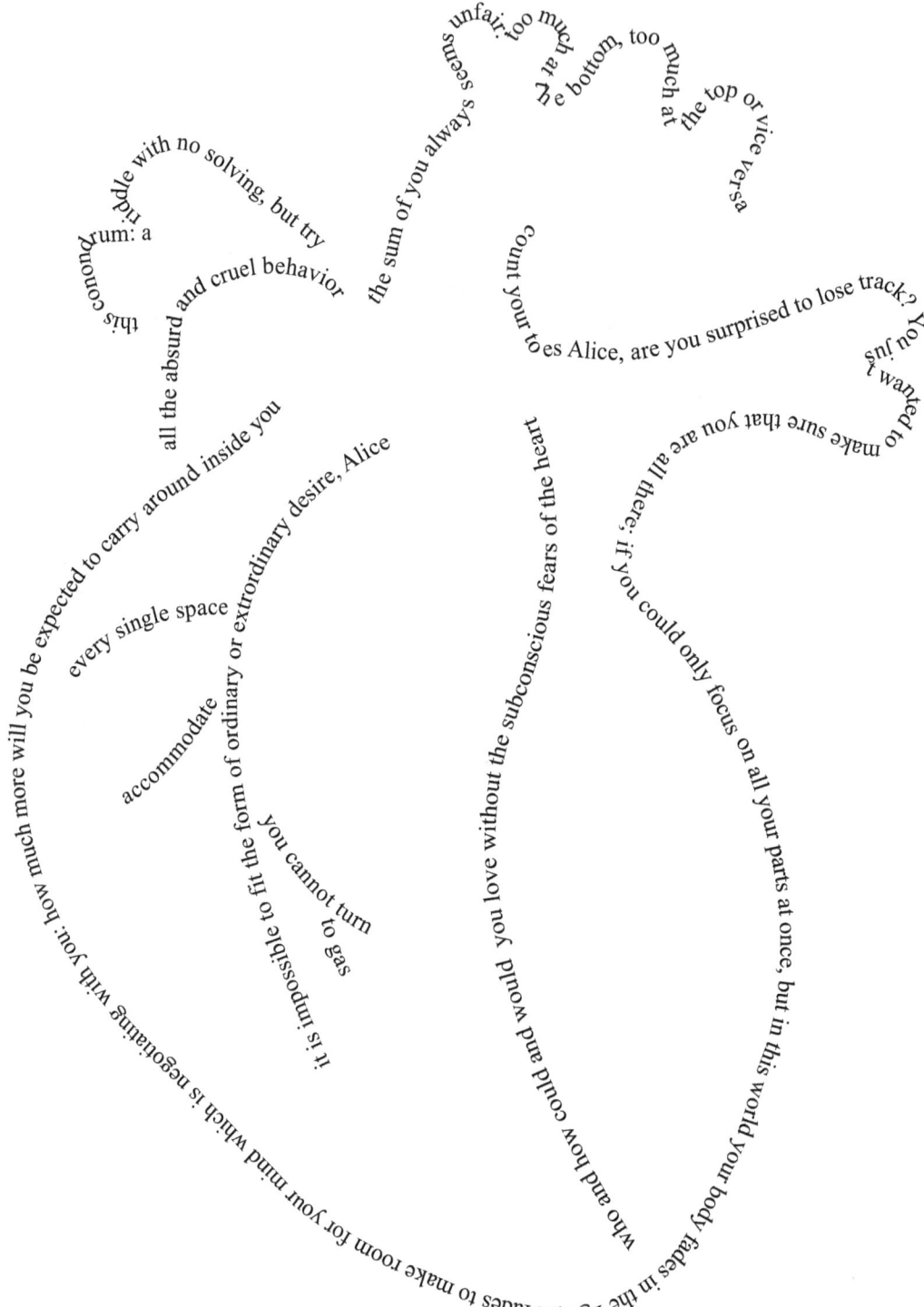

this conundrum: a riddle with no solving, but try
all the absurd and cruel behavior
the sum of you always seems unfair: too much at the bottom, too much at the top or vice versa
count your toes Alice, are you surprised to lose track? You just wanted to make sure that you are all there; if you could only focus on all your parts at once, but in this world your body fades in the light, it fades to make room for your mind which is negotiating with you: how much more will you be expected to carry around inside you
every single space
accommodate
it is impossible to fit the form of ordinary or extrordinary desire, Alice
you cannot turn to gas
who and how could and would you love without the subconscious fears of the heart

Shudder, Clink III

that I will never see all of or touch or kiss but still but still and the nerve it has to sparkle the nerve it has to stretch like a field of turbulent sunflowers I shudder I clink I shrink to think that this is grief dogging me at the crossroads dogging me in my dreams which are the safest world howling to push my legs open to enter me fuck me until I disperse in errant whispers pleadings yes hurt me I would feel anything except this tinderbox blue hot ozone enclosing my life waiting for me to drop like an unpicked thing dry then curdle to juice

IV

Lilliput

When you died, I wanted to know everything about dandelions. The lilliputian flowers: silver,
fiber, bursts, attached to the same base. Each umbrella seed identical to each other.
Mirror after mirror.

We were like this once. Weren't we like this, before the wind? *Please*, tell me we were.

Dearest Sándor,

This is about betrayals. You and I, at our most vulnerable were unbearable disturbances to people we loved. Who wants to return to us? I cannot read Hungarian, but on a piece of paper beside the poem you wrote for your wife, you drew a knife, poised as if to slice through your words. I have known the position of that poem. Love can expel a cloud of dark.

Where do lost things go? What secret hatch do they slide down and does everything reach the sea? Sometimes, when my menstrual blood is thick, I feel as if I am scooting out of my body. I envy the animal that can bare evidence of its sadness and fear. An octopus, when frightened, expels a cloud of dark.

In the history of melanin, Sándor, the Greeks would write their letters to their mistresses, philosophers, and boy loves in the ink from the sac of a cuttlefish: See also, sepia. Into the 1800s, artists drew their figures in it. Humans practically hunted the cuttlefish to extinction.

Perhaps lost things are lost because they want to be. Perhaps lost things are lost because they've been turned loose. Once we say that something is extinct, we find it hiding in the places we dare not look. At this point, desire seems to be something else if it is unrequited. Are we hiding where no one would dare look?

Cliché

It may be cliché to say this, but the way people treat strangers can tell you how they treat themselves and others. I often forget to water my flailing herb garden. I often force my body -- muscles hard from the lactic acid produced in my anxious panics—to be pleasant to my lovers, who expect pleasantries.

Last time I went home to visit, the iyaloja soaked me in a bath of basil, oregano and honey. Her old hands like tubers clenched my limbs, ordering them to release. I told her I was seeing a therapist. She cut her teeth at me, rolled her eyes, and said, "Can they see the enraged demon on your back?"

I want to tell you that I found the letters where you confess to kissing your patients, how you believed it was therapeutic.

Imagine emotion as a color. Now, make that color a lens, and hold it up to the world. Everyone is stained.

I question whether or not the judgment and denials of white men can cure me or anyone for that matter. I found another letter where you told Freud that a mutual patient of yours and his killed herself after you both called her a liar when she said she was raped.

I'm writing to you because we have somehow both ended up in the dimension of unseen things. People avoid us or run through us like rain.

We are so fixed in the imagination, there is no need to acknowledge us anymore. But here is the kicker. We are both here because of the things we can tell. You can tell that you misdiagnosed the world. I can tell the world who is missing from the diagnosis.

Bereft

I hear the sound—air pulsing the eardrum when the room is empty, a wetted finger around the lip of a crystal glass. I cannot tell if it comes from me, like the bellow from a shofar, taking shape in the air, turning into a thing.

Like the second "e" in bereft, the "eh," "eh," "eh" sound of a mouth open in hunger.

Hear it there in the word, the "r," the sour river in the stomach when you haven't had enough. "Reft" comes from the Old English word *reafian*, which means to rob, to plunder; but also the word ruffian is a bitter leaf on this branch, the culprit and the victim living in the word. "Eh," "eh," "eh," the sound of hunger.

People can be holes, my friend. You can drive into them, like lakes, and never be seen or found Again—bobbing to the bottom. A breath, a hollow chamber of air, racing to the top, until it pops.

Minium

I know you are familiar with the feeling of erasure, familiar with the scratch of another's tongue over your name as they forget us. Love and ideas can become undone with accusation; we are both unseamed by lovers who spit into our faces.

I think of all the limpid colors in the world—the illuminating minium, the lead-tin yellows, the bluish whites, all made of poison—crumbling to the floor with their names and origins, despite how lovingly applied. We both expected to be held. We did the work, plied the passion to be a part of the bigger picture.

Scientists found an ancient arachnid with a tail. Lathed in amber, it looked like pinched gold lace, proof that the scorpion is in fact the cousin that kept the tail. What phases of our hurt selves, our forgotten selves, will be preserved in this forest where the trunks of trees cry orange tears? What parts of us will splinter off and survive in our name?

Nightshade

It is true: Much more can exist in the mind than in the world. What happens in fantasy can be more horrible. Darkness hops out of us fully grown and marches into the material.

All of our freckled horses flood into a field of nightshade.

It is possible for the body to slip the mind as a hand slips a glove. It twists and bends away from our dark imaginings.

And vice versa: The mind may slip the deteriorating body, a reptilian thing, moulting, a light going out in a bedroom window and never turning on again.

I count out my grief, my currency in life for as long as I can remember.

Honey

Like you, I want my insides all outside. In all things, I agree with and abide by love—which I am sure you will agree is fickle. I had a thought, dearest friend, about surgery—how some problems can only be fixed through shameless messes and disregard for fear.

I am a Black girl with palms blatantly towards the sky, waiting for some love to come down like honey. I have spilled my desperation openly to those who would define this act as unstable and irresponsible—and maybe it is.

I carry my loss, tucked between my thighs like a skirt, throwing roses to strangers. But you know acting out like this begins much, much earlier.

You too, have been slighted and pushed into the light as a reckless hysteric because you wanted and touched the embarrassment of wanting. You watched the one you wanted walk away, even as you called his name.

Friend, I have tried to go to that river to fill my bucket, but it dries up before me every time. Why won't it give? You, who died of thirst with sugar on your tongue, how will I ever survive?

Dream with Orchid

By the time you read this, I will remember this dream in a different fashion. But in my dream, suddenly, I was standing beside an orchid.

The pearlescent bluewhite pooling to the tyrian purple center, mimicking arousal. This, I envied. So, for hundreds of years I stood still beside the flower, striking poses, until one day my body took on the flower's colors and my legs grew subtle fins to match the leathery petals.

I became beautiful.

I became so akin to the orchid that it became my name.

I think of all the things I wanted from love, but never received before becoming the orchid.

Then I think of all the forms I will never take now that I have mastered this imitation.

Black Girl Notes on/to Sándor Ferenczi

July 2014. West Palm Beach, FL

You would have appreciated the mock documentary. My mother and I sat on the couch, our bodies like nautilus chambers, me, curved smaller against her curving. The CGI[1] enlivened the slick black bodies of merpeople. The idea was that humans did not plop from a tree, like some burden of fruit, but that they writhed onto land, and after many sufferings, learned to take in air.

No wonder we have such a hard time, why we linger at water's edge. The backlash was total. The mock documentary was misleading, too real. My mother was watching it for the merpeople. But the idea rested in me like bread on water, the tiny minnows of my thought picking away. If this is at all plausible, the whole white kernel of the world becomes wrong, even you.

February 2015. Bronx, NYC

Let's be clear. You and your teacher, Freud, were rampant racists. I don't even exist in your catalog of human specimens. I think I am at a point now that I can talk to you because if you were reincarnated in my kitchen you would take the form of some purple jelly slopped from my sandwich —as if you were part of a scene from *Hellraiser*. I know at least five mothers who live on my floor who can re-educate you. I suspect that your apprenticeship to Freud was fraught, that he was sure of my inferiority, but that you were in it for the funding. Your notions of water origin and vagina-centered worlds got you laughed out of the academy. Still, that's a start.

May 2015. Macon, GA

I am at a bar where the wood is sticky like my tongue. I am stomping my feet and the lyrics to the bluegrass come from my mouth like bolts of yellow silk evaporating. I sway like a plum coral fan planted on a reef. And I can't help but recall what you say about sex. That it is fueled by needing to cool off, return to water. That we push and grunt our way into each other, grapple with our skins, trying to go home. *Etútú*. Sándor, that means "to cool" in Yoruba. It is what my auntie's tongue clicks out when we call our godfolk from the water.

January 2016. Savannah, GA

I love cities where the living know their place. All my folks come from cities like that. Entire places necklaced with ocean, choked with salt that conducts the dead. I am explaining you to my auntie who draws people's blood for a living. Her scrubs are decorated in little spots of coral. Suddenly my everything below my belly button is like a ruffled yellow bird, chirping, and popping up and down like a hot seed in an oily pan. I stop and drink a glass of water, say to my aunt that I want to go swimming. She replies, "But baby, you know it is jellyfish season."

---

1 Computer generated imagery

September 2016. Pittsburgh, PA

The purpose of your letters to Freud can be boiled down to your shouting, "Please believe me!" But with all the attention he was getting, you were hardly worth the trouble. I have never seen anyone give up power for the love of an individual. So much for friendship and scholarly attachments. My professor and I talk during break about taking your theories in essence and reviving them through a Black feminist queer lens. In short, someone needs to tell you about your sorry ass, about what you really meant to say all that time.

Flay

It is more difficult than you think to flay belief from the self, Sándor. The skim on a soup, the light chinking off the parabola of a wave. You are not the first or only one to have said that the ocean is a womb is an ocean. You said that when we were thrown to the land that we kept the water between our hip bones. Grieving is trying to put something in the place of the lost object.

We used to believe in our gills. Sanity isn't always necessary for survival. On the contrary. You crossed the line. You married psychology, science (or it was at the time), and your intuition. You whittled them all down to mythologies.

They called you crazy. They called us animals. They called us, the women, animals. They disowned us from reason, too.

Lycanthropy

What is it called, Sándor, when a thing wants to be anything besides what it is? The primal fear we have as humans of the heavy sea. Just in my lifetime, one island disappeared from the waves and two new islands emerged and birds descended.

I have the inclination to moult, to shed. In lucid moments, I can smell my skin loosening, taking on feathers or scales. Birds and humans, feathers and hair, arose from the same mutation in a beast that, once on land, grew tired of the weight of its scales. One more dimple in the chromosome and we could have flown.

Language isn't sufficient anymore. I put a word in my mouth and turn it, say purple when I mean no. I need more ways to say. This human-animal body can only imitate so many things—can only be so specific. I will a transformation where the urge to protect myself like a predator is second nature. I want the toil of a free beast, a wild horse, only grazing and running. I dream of being made for a desert night: sharp, shelled, glowing, ready. I want this amness but inside of an arctic sea creature, a shark that lives for 500 years, knowing time the way the shark knows it: chill, alarming, in infinite blues and a choke of greens.

Write back to me.

Vacation

This house is old and dusty with heavy stone walls; the roof tiled in ultramarine to keep cool. The night moves like a damp purple sheet hung out to dry.

The fishermen spark flames in lanterns hanging from their boats—thin and loud—like petals from a flor de paraiso. Their boat's spines divide the water, and just beyond the bay, a wave bobs them playfully.

You are right, it is tiring to always write about loneliness. It is tough to carry one long-feathered wing grown painfully on the back.

I have passed my life wanting and waiting for the things I want to want me back; my hands are always empty. I need more and more reasons and I cannot bear to be put down again.

Desire looks like traveling over indeterminate sky and water, getting lost in a mirror, hoping to return with something to satiate you for a while.

And really, there is no more to tell. Not getting what you want is simple, blunt, and maddening. And no, the sun will not fail to come up on account of it.

Actuary

Our lack is an opening to the basement of who we are, Sándor. Things crawl in, avoiding the flood. They root among our roots. So, how dare it be asked *what's to fear?*

It is prudent that we look before the water rises, intimately know the tender yet armored Arachnid, pregnant with young identical to her. She will burst, she will bite.

Who made this? What hands, probably without intention, failed every piece of us scaffolded above this hole? What hands were so illiterate to their palms

that they could not prepare us for our drowning? We stand and try to name the lovely hex of creatures that have crawled in, taking an account of ourselves.

We are up to our necks; the basement around us now a sinkhole, now a part of the wilderness. Our only fault is that we built so high without knowing it was too late.

Respite: We can and may have to abandon it all. We don't have to do this—but wait, the water....

Shudder, Clink IV

then wetness that the air sucks up and out then rain over some ocean that at this point the name doesn't matter I shudder I clink I shrink to think that this is grief who will be dead by the time I am old who will join the chorus of protection that I schlep into every room that every witchy woman curls from how many panopticon ghost eyes will witness all of my failures I am the worst at being a "woman" that a "man" can love I am the worst at reciprocations that cut unearned meat from my desire to do what I wish no one wants a boy in their house not even fathers no one wants a daughter

V

Lilliput

When you died, I wanted to know
everything about dandelions.
The lilliputian flowers: silver, fiber,
bursts, attached to the same base.
Each umbrella seed identical
to one another.
Mirror after mirror.

We were like this once.
Weren't we like this,
before the wind?
Please, tell me we were.

Hex

Araucaria[1]
Araucaria[2]
Monkey Puzzle[3]

Bougainvillea[4]
Bougainvillea[5]
Bougainvillea[6]

Bruise[7]
Bruise[8]
Bruise[9]

[1] The fibrous teeth of the trunk, the copper body like a godbig snake.
[2] The finger-thick, green needles; good for whipping the legs of your older brothers.
[3] This was the tree's name until a Nancy Morejón poem told me different. See also araucaria.
[4] Fuchsia creeper, bushel of tongues, all over the walls.
[5] A photo in which it was wound in my great grandmother's hair, a wreath of paper-thin tongues.
[6] It barely touched my mother's face. Her cheek swelled, then her skin flaked.
[7] Like a daisy chain around the neck. Like a sign of love.
[8] An eclipse, a bad omen, shadowing over; a shiner.
[9] A contusion : a slug : pour salt all around you.

Drawing Lesson #34: A Home

Room #1

See a mountain. Crevices forever frozen in molten
explosion. The rhythm of liquid locked in pouring.
Rain pattering from the roof. Here this mountain
will never be despised, it can breathe brown and gray, free
from its natural enemy. Perhaps I am writing about my
body. Like a mountain, it has been considered
uncrossable, mysterious, an eyesore,
something to blow apart.

Room #2

A rock. In the middle there, a little magpie stone.
The white walls—yellowwhite—surround it, stay
kneeled about it in begging. It is a stilled piece
of ocean. Religious men used to think the human
body was made of millions of tiny human-shaped units.
People died—accused of their homunculus being unruly.
If we can believe that, we can believe this rock
can drown whoever enters here at any second.

Room #3

The words *I don't understand* and *I hatc* livc here
as a couple. It is a studio apartment, really not enough
room. One gets mad when the other doesn't do the dishes.
One masturbates while lying next to the other, tries
to be as quiet as possible during climax. I wonder how
they met, how they stand it, living together.

Room #4

This is my room for happy things. I only come here alone.
When I brought other people here, shit went missing.
I will list some of the things here so you can get an idea,
since you can't come in: a necklace that belonged
to my mother, a kiddie pool with holes in it, some two
dollar bills, the baby teeth of my nieces and nephews, and
the black velvet dress with paste jewels on it that I always
wanted, but never got. There is not much continuity
in these things. But if happiness was intelligible
we'd all have a room.

Room #5

I keep a lot of memories here. They are doppelgängers.
They wear masks and caper around. They are tricky.
They don't need much feeding. I have a suspicion
that they may eat one another. What level of hell is it where
a person rips themselves apart flesh from flesh only
to find their body whole again? Last I opened this room,
all of them had transformed into a party of excited blue jays.
They toppled in flight before me.

Room #6

Things I don't want or need go in here. It is embarrassing
what isn't here. I am learning to economize. Silverware
used to be made of bamboo and other natural materials.
We could fill a smaller planet with cutlery now.
I have a question about disposability that I have trouble
putting together, and it starts in this room.

Room #7

Once someone told me they have a room full of their dreams.
I told them that was a bad design idea. They asked me why,
and I said because everyone has one and all of them have
the same shit, to be honest. They wanted to know what
I would do with my dream room. I tell them
that it is where I would keep some dirt and a window.
I would lie there in the eternal square of light and think of nothing.

Erasure

I will draw my own forest and I will walk into it.
Like a hand shaking pieces of bone, I will rattle and vibrate,

then dissolve into the sky.

I want to paint a red mountain, draw the treeline, and go stand
pale and fleshy as a sycamore in the middle there,
with my arms above my head, and you will say,
Ah—there is a petrified tree.

But this is my forest. I have drawn it
and there is no way in, but through
this vanishing point,
which I am now
erasing.

Empty Space

"I think that a poem about empty space would be sublime."
Georg Christoph Lichtenberg

And an emptiness sublime is what would come to be
should god clear its throat.

I dream the universe is god's wet mouth, constantly open,
and everything inside a swirling bacteria.

An emptiness sublime: Imagine drawing the word house, then erasing
it with everything it could mean and contain.

The stars do come down, they do reach our fingers from their unfathomable
combustions. They do, like us, become stones and dirt.

I want this for my body: a light so light, a black so black that corners
become invisible, and even I become invisible.

Erasing can be an easement, a taking off of hands, not having
or wanting or needing to hold anything.

I think of how when people speak of joy, they seem self-conscious,
apologizing for their enthusiasm, trying not to disturb others.

Men have been writing about going to the moon for so long: on a rope,
on a plant, in a bucket. When they make it, there is someone to call it a lie.

It isn't everyone who reads past *Inferno*; most people are content
to paint their rooms white.

It seems that a person who stops and gazes at anything for too long,
without taking a bit for themselves, is strange.

Milagro, Carry Your Altar

all over our bodies / are pieces / of other bodies / dangling organs / of thin metal / small spiritual donors / my great grandmother gives me a silver brain to hang from my ear—for my brother / she says / a long finger / calcified still at the knuckle / vining rod: a grave : water : gold : shame / family joke: a silver tongue near the ear

so that a husband's

lies are heard sweetly / we all wore

gold eyes from red string on our necks / when my aunt got glaucoma / her "green eyes" / we prayed / i have four brothers / that i could wear gold impressions of their whole bodies / on maps / that they may always arrive at home safely

the more

dire the need / more expensive metal / how much can be afforded / even god needs a little

witchcraft

mother wears a tiny gold punched uterus / a child curled inside / a small coma

that i could wear a forest of gold

scraps / that i could jangle with begging

to make him kneel / i touch my gold ear charm / that i wear for god

Raising a Wolf

She held me in her arms, declared
that I would not be raised as a girl.

Leaving me hungry to persuade me
to hunt alone and for myself.

One raises a wolf by demonstrating the necessity
of being raised as a wolf.

Thin skin, worn like paper erased of words,
Tides in her forearm; tight-tight, smothered.

I bit my mother.
Told her that I refused her sorrow.

Howl at the pain of new incisors, crescent
moons in the mouth, bristle to a touch.

A mouth full of sand, in my teeth, wetting
with saliva, is no way to feed myself.

Opaline, god's tooth blue, ovular beads, pawed
from a riverbank's lung, wanting to swallow them.

The first tongue ever, slipped, like a letter
through a slot into my mouth which I also bit.

A cultivated desire for wilderness to my back
instead of shelter, the sky won't fall in my lifetime.

I was taught that the anecdote for female fragility
is another fragility—to bite everything in sight.

Akhmatova as Drawn by Modigliani

You remember him

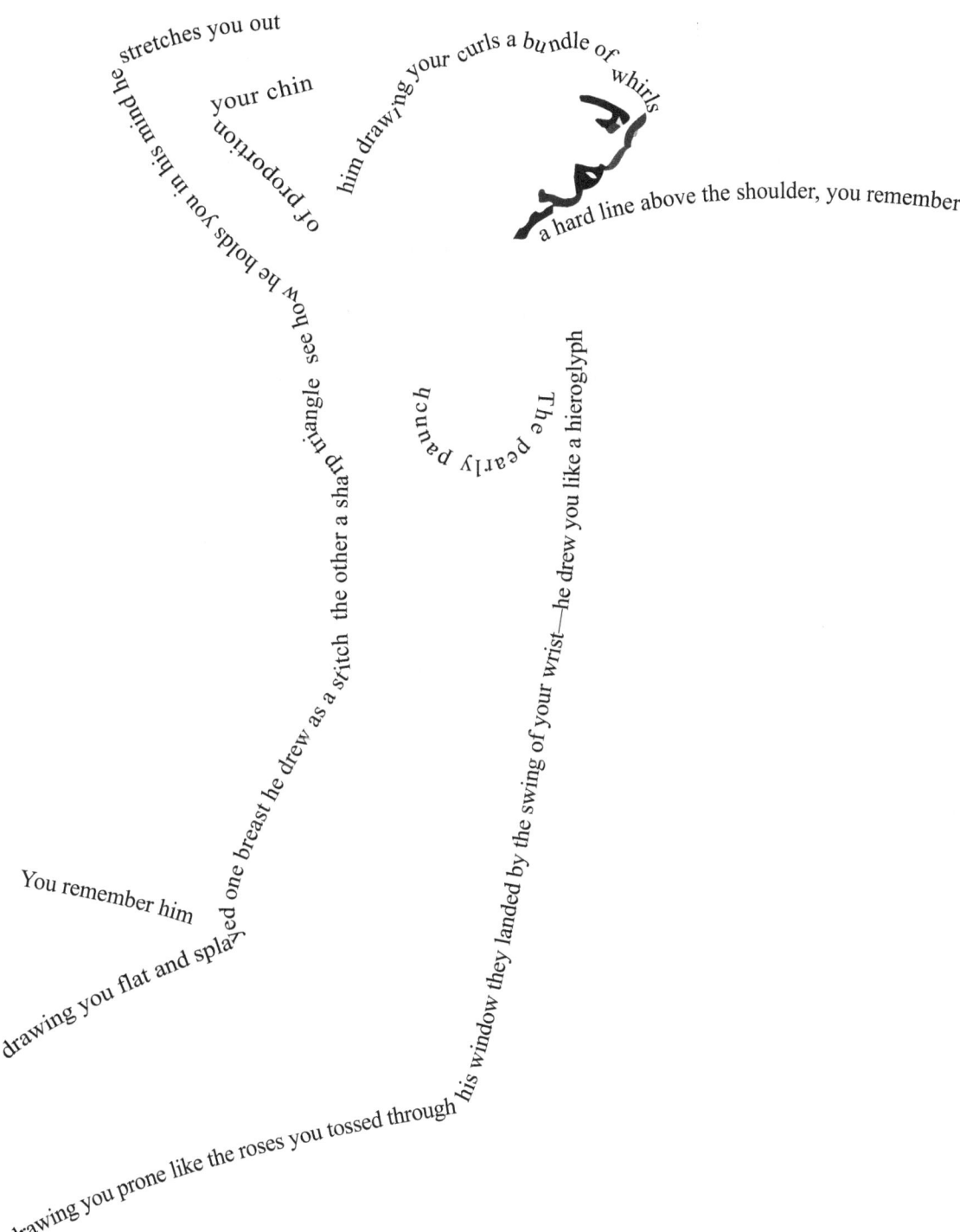

drawing you flat and splayed one breast he drew as a stitch the other a sharp triangle see how he holds you in his mind he stretches you out

your chin

of proportion

him drawing your curls a bundle of whirls

a hard line above the shoulder, you remember

The pearly paunch

drawing you prone like the roses you tossed through his window they landed by the swing of your wrist—he drew you like a hieroglyph

Dear Mountain,

I am foraging within your pleats, picking at your bruisable flowers for sustenance. I am a poor stranger in this field where you cut sharply upward from flatness. You are a wrinkle in the land I cannot see past or across.

But, let me stop here. You never wanted to be a mountain—you never asked for that. Let me be fair.

I will begin again by saying that today I read somewhere that when a person loses something, it was their intention—consciously or unconsciously—to be rid of it. In my mind the former is equal to a haunting and the latter is equal to a haunting.

I am not a receipt in your pocket that you have convinced yourself you will eventually need and so keep.

Then there is this mountain against which I am so small that there is no difference in size between me and a sprig of grass.

The landscape changes so quickly with you by my side; suddenly things are two dimensional and I feel as if I am sliding down a verticality.

Maybe we meant for each other to be like hats taken by the wind, dervishing away, loping. Sweat rings about the brims.

And now, I am in a tiny boat in the middle of a mirror that is sometimes called the ocean. Have you ever been in a boat on a clear black night? It is nothing like being in a star shower.

But from this boat I look behind to see your lantern swinging along the shore, a direction.

But by now, dear Mountain, I am so tired, that I think I will just rest here and look towards nothing, my back to your light.

Pleats

mountains are on the female spectrum

married to that idea
if people are still

nothing "new" is going to happen here at best it hasn't been heard

many different things based on the same model here is a pencil ready to draw a mountain

I draw the pleats like vulva because you should see a skirt those things because

insurmountable

suddenly some things aren't very true I just want to draw

a space

I can walk into and be done there isn't really a point in

just to fashion

all this

an escape

drawing

light is all over the place like spilled olive oil because—the vulva the mountain because

virtuosity in the depths is just my idea of where the sun is and isn't

for a long time at best everyone's self conscious will render

hatch into a useful solitude

my pencil is fixed let's avoid the metaphor where the page is the universe

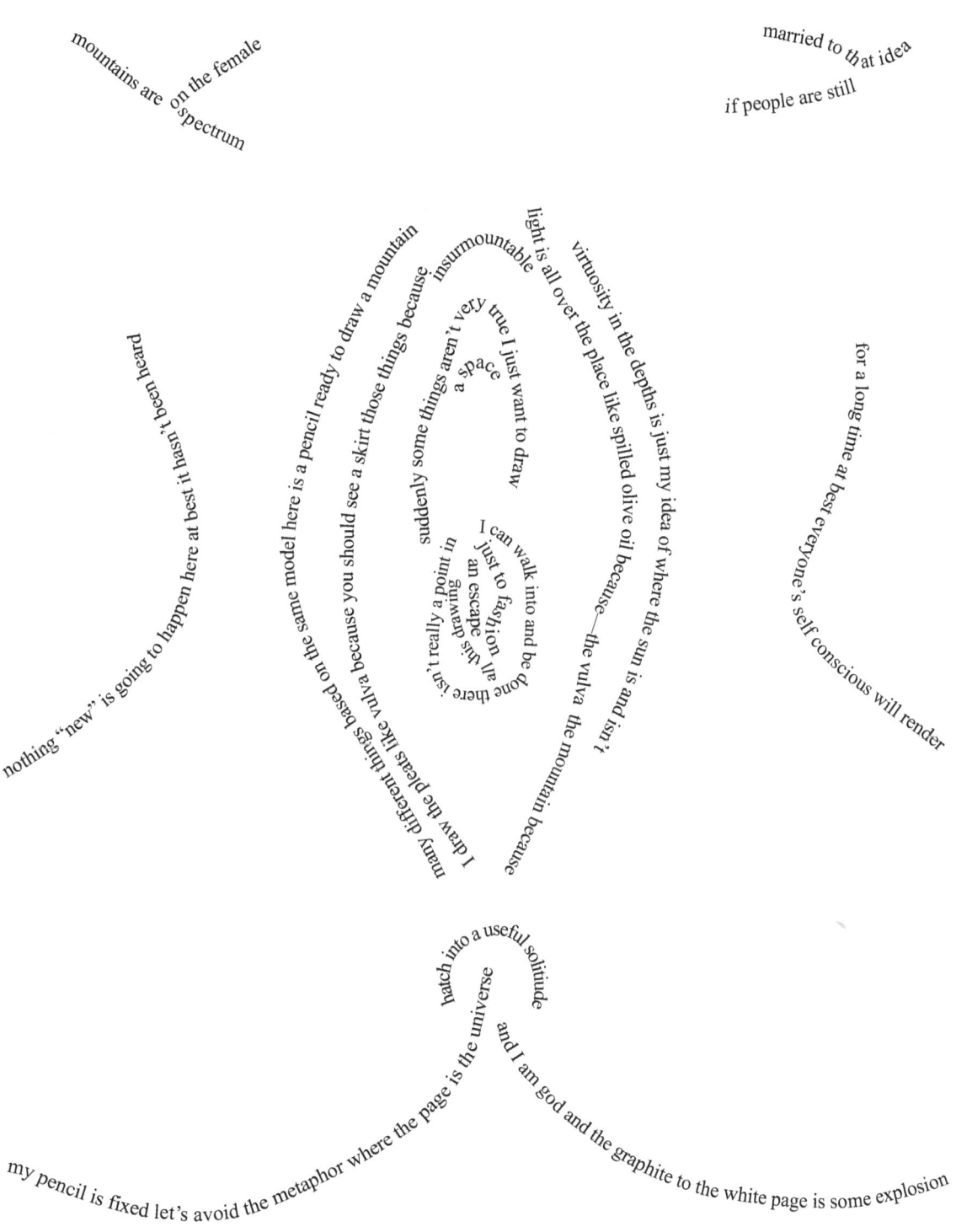

and I am god and the graphite to the white page is some explosion

Shudder, Clink V

in their house that is unpluckable and refuses to become an adornment I shudder I clink I shrink to think that this is grief It takes too many mythologies to explain too many stories back-hacked into that ur-text of human desire that reads one word escape since we threw up our hands as a symbol of goodbye we have been trying to catalog loss to things we cannot hold in our palms or lock in cages: it was not the tiger it was not the unknown bacterium it was the hunger other thing's will to live and our own that do us in I shudder I clink I shrink to think that this is grief

Waiting

The wheels grind—forward forward—the locomotive traces the frayed Hudson's hem. Water lines from the last natural violence mark where the long mouth overflowed with itself. Sometimes you just need to yell. Just to go—only to say you were gone. Getting on this not-so-modern beast, that still does not know to slow at hairpin curves. Two small girls caterwaul down the aisles, bumping the seats, their mother looking on disapprovingly, the grandmother looking over her daughter, daring her to protest. The weather against the window is cold enough for a light coat, but humid enough to sweat through it. A swallow quavers in a dagger of light between luggage. Strangers descend, asundered from the remains of their conversations. *You really find out a lot about relationships once you cut the person off, you know, if you don't feel you suffer without them, you never needed them to begin with.... What a waste of time.* The man across, handsome and aging, discreetly counts the watermelons on his shirt then with a dry twist, removes his wedding ring, slumps down until we are eye level. *It is times like this I wish the ride would never end,* he says. *Somehow it is comforting not to have be anywhere.* Nodding, I think of all the undetonated metal weapons at the bottom of the oceans. For some reason, I think about this train getting lost like so many others that tried to push through the folded ice palms of Siberia. After I disembark, all that will be left is the grease halo from my forehead. I think of all the people who have never ever returned from places simply named *do-not-go-there.*

About the Author

Jessica Lanay, originally from Key West, Florida, is a poet, librettist, short fiction writer, and art writer. Her work focuses on architectures of interiority, and escapism. Her poetry has appeared in *The COMMON, Poet Lore, Prairie Schooner, Indiana Review, [PANK],* and other publications. Her short fiction was published in Tahoma Literary Review, Duende, and Black Candies: A Journal of Literary Horror. Her art writing can be found in BOMB Magazine. She wrote the libretto for *Virgula Divina,* an opera composed by Karen Brown, to premiere in February 2020. She is a fellow of Cave Canem, Callaloo, and Kimbilio.

www.ingramcontent.com/pod-product-compliance
Lightning Source LLC
Chambersburg PA
CBHW081329190426
43193CB00044B/2900
* 9 7 8 0 9 4 0 7 1 3 2 8 4 *